the flower shop ^{SM}

Volume 1
A Companion Book
To The Television Series with Host
Phil Easter

written by M.L. Boyle

WCN Productions

Winter Park, Florida

Photographer: Theodore Flagg

Copyright © 1987 by WCN Productions

WCN Productions
Winter Park, Florida 32789

International Standard Book Number   0-943735-00-9
Printed in the United States of America
87 88 89 90   10 9 8 7 6 5 4 3 2 1

Contents

Acknowledgments

Because the writing of scripts for *the flower shop* fell to my associate, Joe Hall, and me, it followed that this book be similarly scripted. The challenge was this: to create both a television series and a companion book with sound, accurate floral design information. The job of compiling such information could only be accomplished by calling on acknowledged experts within the floral industry itself. To that end, I sought recognized men and women with solid credentials to supply the technical data. I also encouraged these professionals to impart some of their extensive knowledge and advice related to floral design. They all responded unselfishly by offering floral resource information that they felt applicable to our concept. I would like to thank these experts who so kindly supplied resource and design information. They are noted in the chapters in which they advised according to their particular expertise.

To further guarantee the accuracy and validity of the information presented in this book, I wished to establish an ad hoc advisory committee. The problem was how to determine who should serve on such a committee? It seemed sensible to ask as many people in the floral industry as possible who he or she would recommend for such a position. In asking this question of numerous floral designers, floral company executives, floral design teachers, and product representatives, three names were continually mentioned. On that basis, I asked those three individuals for their help in this endeavor. They kindly accepted.

Serving as Chairman of the Committee is Dr. Henry M. Cathey, Director of the U.S. National Arboretum in Washington, D.C., a research and education facility of the Agricultural Research Service, U.S. Department of Agriculture. Dr. Cathy is a renowned featured speaker and writer in the field of horticulture.

Ms. Frankie Shelton and Mr. Ralph Null, also serve as committee members. Sincere thanks to them for accepting the charge of making sure that this book presents accurate information to the reader.

Phil Easter is responsible for much of the information found in the chapters of this book. He is also a resource designer and he has the final word on all the information presented in the series and in this book. His expertise is an invaluable addition to this entire effort. It is not possible to describe the satisfaction that we all found in working with such an inspired and dedicated individual; his professionalism is without peer. His integrity is admired by all who know him.

I would also like to thank the following:

Joe Hall: Director, Co-producer, and Co-author of the television series. Mr. Hall has been associated with WCN Productions since its early days. He is a professor of radio and television production at the University of Central Florida. Mr. Hall brings experience and abilities to our company that are too numerous to mention. He plays a major role in creating and implementing all of the company television projects. I sincerely hope that we will continue to collaborate on video projects. It is my real privilege to work with him.

Peggy Horne: Floral Design Coordinator for the series, Ms. Horne was in charge of bringing together all of the flowers and materials for the designs shown on the air and in this book. She coordinated all of the floral arrangements seen on the series and in this book, including simulating the floral aspects of an actual flower shop for our television production. Additionally, Ms. Horne supplied the initial information that brought WCN Productions together with floral experts across the country.

Jason McCollum: In addition to acting in the capacity of resource designer (Chapter 11, "Eloquence of Flowers"), Mr. McCollum was the floral arranger for the photographs found in this book. It was his job to transform each resource expert's designs into "reality." His extensive talents in this area are seen in the photographs of this book.

Keiko Nemeth: Associate producer of the series. Ms. Nemeth acted as set designer, and handled the many functions that fall under the "Associate producer" label. She worked with Director Joe Hall on the initial design of the two sets (Ms. Nemeth is an artist in her own right), and orchestrated the designs for the sets. Her artistic abilities are obviously illustrated by her ability to effect varied set themes on a miniscule budget. She and Ms. Horne worked closely together.

Lastly, I would like to thank **Michele Cannon**, *to whom this book is dedicated.* Michele is Assistant to the producer, a phrase that may have many meanings. In this case, it means dear friend and long-time associate who has, by means of long hours, expert advice, exceptional talent, and an unquestioned loyalty, helped to build our company. Officially she now holds the position of Controller of our corporation. Unofficially, she is a human "rock." Without her we would not have this book, or series. I am proud to be associated with Michele Cannon, and pleased to thank her in print for her unswerving support and presence.

Editorial assistance was provided by Mr. Randy Knight, Horticultural Consultant, Orlando, Florida, and Mr. Raymond Morris, Floral Columnist (Palm Beach Daily News) and Designer, Palm Beach, Florida.

This publication was only possible due to the excellent endeavors of all of the aforementioned people. They all have my sincere thanks and appreciation.

M. L. Boyle

Special Thanks

WCN Productions expresses its appreciation to Wholesale Florists and Florist Suppliers of America, whose major funding made possible *the flower shop* television series.

With us, WF & FSA encourages American viewers to bring the joy of flowers into their lives on a daily basis.

Additional funding provided by member florists of FTD

and

Armellini Express Lines.

Here host Phil Easter discusses a scene with Director
Joe Hall and Executive Producer M.L. Boyle

About the Host

Phil Easter has been actively involved in the floral industry for 30 years. Phil has a B.S. in Floriculture from Colorado State University and has attended the American Floral Arts School. He is a member of the American Academy of Florists, American Institute of Floral Designers, and Professional Floral Commentators International.

Phil has extensive experience in marketing flowers. He operated a successful retail flower shop for nearly 20 years, and now supervises a team of designers and merchandisers of silk and dried floral arrangements for Caffco International. As Director of Industry Communications, Phil maintains active contact with the retail and wholesale floral industry.

As a veteran of over 200 programs and demonstrations for civic groups, garden clubs, and industry symposiums, Phil has demonstrated his ability in floral design instruction. He has taught floral design for the Montgomery, Alabama public school district adult education program and heads an Artist in Residence Program for the American Institute of Floral Designers.

the flower shop has benefited greatly from the proven expertise of Phil Easter. We are pleased that he has chosen to share his years of experience with our audience.

Materials and Usage

Floral Foam: Floral foam comes in two basic types: one, generally green in color, has a water-holding capability and is used when designing with fresh materials. The second type, dry floral foam, is tan or brown. It is used when no water reservoir is necessary; when working with dried materials and silk flowers, for instance. These two types of foam are not interchangeable, so be careful to select the right type for your arrangement.

Floral foam comes in brick form and can easily be cut with a knife. Cut it to the size and shape of your container. Both water-holding and dry types can be snugly secured to the container with the use of floral adhesive tape. (Many of the commonly used design containers come with prongs or evenly-spaced spikes that hold the foam securely in place. In this case, floral adhesive tape may not be necessary.)

Water-holding foam must be fully saturated before you place it in the container and begin the arrangement. The foam should be immersed in a solution of warm water (100-115°) to which the prescribed amount of floral preservative has been added. A few minutes of soaking in this solution should suffice. Full saturation has occured when air bubbles stop coming out of the foam. If, when cutting the foam to fit the container, you find any dry area in the center of the block, re-soak the foam. Any dryness in the foam will undermine its purpose of continually supplying moisture to the fresh materials with which it comes in contact. When fitting the foam to the container, make sure to leave adequate space on all sides as a reservoir for a generous water supply. The foam, as a rule, should extend upward approximately ½" to 1" above the rim. Before anchoring with a floral adhesive tape, dry the sides and lip of the container for good adhesion; this prevents the block from moving in the container as you work on the arrangement.

Basic Types of Flowers: It is important to have basic information about flower types to aid in our enjoyment of flower arranging. Type classification is primarily established by the way the materials are used in arrangements. As we work more with flowers, however, we'll realize that their usage may change, depending upon the specific arrangment being considered. The basic types of flowers are:

Focal or Mass Flowers: carnations, roses, standard chrysanthemums, etc.
Line or Spike Flowers: gladioli, snapdragons, bells of Ireland, Scotch broom, pussy willows, etc.
Filler Flowers: baby's breath, statice, wax flowers
Form Flowers with strong or outstanding shapes: orchids, anthuriums, birds of paradise, irises

Spray Flowers: pompon chrysanthemums, miniature carnations

Accent Flowers: miniature roses (and other flowers being used as accents because of their size, shape, or color.)

Necessary Tools: As in any endeavor, working with flowers is much easier and more enjoyable if the proper tools are used. This is especially true when working with fresh materials. Working with the proper tools will make your learning experience easier and, in most cases, will extend the life of fresh flowers.

The most important tool when working with fresh materials is a good, sharp, well-balanced knife. Several types of knives are available for floral designing. Some have stationary blades while others fold, similar to a pocket knife. While each designer finds the best knife according to his or her preference, the most important quality of a good knife is how well it holds an edge.

Other basic tools needed for designing with fresh materials are three types of scissors or shears. One type, preferably with a serrated edge, is capable of cutting chicken wire, florist's wire, etc. The second type is used only when cutting soft materials such as foliages and ribbons. The third type of shear is used primarily to cut flower stems without causing damage to the stems. This is especially important since recent research focuses on prolonging flower life by cutting stems under water.

When we begin to work with nonperishable materials (fabric flowers, dried materials), the tools are a bit different. While a knife is still important, a good pair of wire cutters is essential. You may be tempted to use household or conventional cutters. Resist that temptation and purchase something suitable to the task. You will also find frequent use for a pair of needle-nosed pliers; and believe it or not, an ice pick is another household tool that often comes in handy.

Before we leave the discussion of proper tools, let's take some time to learn to use a knife properly, and without fear. The following instructions are for a right-handed individual.

1. Holding your left hand in front of you, palm upwards, place the flower stem in your hand with the flower head away from you and the base of the stem toward you. Grasp the stem firmly.
2. Grasp the knife in your right hand with the second digit of the index finger resting against the back edge of the blade.
3. As you move your left hand and the stem away from you, pull the cutting edge of the knife toward you with the blade at a 45° angle against the stem. Continue pushing away with your left hand, pulling toward you with your right hand and holding the stem against the cutting edge of the knife with your right thumb. Be sure to move your entire right hand and arm as you cut, reducing the chance that your right thumb might be cut by the knife as it

passes through the stem. Do not press the stem against the cutting edge of the blade so hard that the stem bends or is pinched between your thumb and the knife.

The goal is to achieve a good, clean cut without damaging the flower stem. A pinched or bent stem will greatly reduce the flower's ability to draw water up the stem to the flower head.

Practice the above procedure a number of times on left-over portions of stems until you begin to feel more comfortable using the knife and are making good, clean cuts on the stem.

Care and Handling of Tools: Buying high quality florist tools is a wise investment if you are to enjoy flower arranging. Protect that investment by exercising proper use and care of your tools each time you use them.

USE

1. Never use your tools to do a job they weren't designed to do: don't dig up plants or hammer objects with tools designed only for cutting.
2. Never use a scissors designed for soft materials to cut wire stems; use a wire stem cutter, or appropriate serrated scissors.
3. Use the proper scissors at all times. Ribbon cutting shears are just for that purpose, cutting ribbons and other soft materials that will not damage the cutting edge.
4. Never try to create more cutting pressure on a tool than you can create with your hand. Hammering on the handles or using the tool as a pry bar creates a very dangerous situation as the tool can break and cause serious harm.
5. Never expose your cutting tools to excessive heat as heat can change the temper of the blades.
6. Don't rock the tool from side to side trying to cut an object. Use a tool with proper leverage and cutting ability.
7. Never use the tips of your cutting tools as a pry.
8. Never use cutting tools as a hammer. Any tool that is cracked, broken, or sprung should be discarded for safety's sake.
9. Always store your cutting tools out of the reach of small children.

CARE

1. Keep your tools clean and free of moisture by promptly wiping off dirt and water after each use and before they are stored.
2. If you allowed dirt and sap to build up on the blades, clean this buildup with a light solvent such as mineral spirits so that the blades will remain in good condition.
3. Put an occasional drop of household oil on the joint. To store tools for any

length of time, it's advisable to leave a light film of oil on the insides of the blades.

If you use and care for them properly, quality tools should maintain sharp cutting edges for many years. If you feel that a tool needs sharpening, it is recommended that it be taken to a professional sharpening service to ensure that the original angle of the blade and beveled cutting edge is maintained.

Floral tool use and care information supplied by:
CLAUSS Cutlery Company, Fremont, Ohio.

Overview of Floral Design

Since the beginning of time man has been drawn to the beauties of nature. The creation story first places man in a garden. Of course, man first depended on nature to meet the basic needs of food, clothing, and shelter. However, when civilization progressed to the point where survival was no longer the major concern, creative expression began to develop.

In looking at ancient civilizations, such as those of Egypt, Greece, Rome, and the Orient, we find that flowers played a very significant role. Artifacts and archaeologic finds from these cultures point out the importance of flowers and floral decorating. If we are trying to determine why flowers are important to our culture, we turn to the history books. They tell us that flowers were originally available only for those of means. With the Industrial Revolution and the increase of the working class, the growth in individual homes and gardens allowed flowers to become available to society in general.

In order to understand the basics of design in flower arranging, we must again turn to the history books and look at a thumbnail sketch of the history of this art. Simply stated, it can be divided into three parts: Oriental, European, and American.

The Oriental or Eastern type of arranging goes back over 2000 years and concerns itself with mathematical precision and interpretation of nature. Anything that has survived for that long, without change, must be good!

The European or Western type of arranging is sometimes called Williamsburg, Victorian, or Colonial. It concerns itself with a mass of flowers, and a mass of color.

The American style takes a little from the East and a little from the West. It has developed into what we call the "contemporary" style of arranging. Here we have the color of the West and the line of the East, minus all the rules and restrictions usually encountered with those methods. It gives us freedom to create, but we must follow a few basic rules.

Order and organization are needed to create a good design. You can compare a floral design to a blueprint. If you set reasonable objectives for yourself, an effective end result will be achieved by using guidelines, correct tools, and applicable principles.

Flowers placed in a vase without any particular design are beautiful for the simple reason that flowers, in themselves, are beautiful. The same flowers, arranged

Within the category of balance, arrangements can be symmetrical or asymmetrical. The symmetrical design is usually balanced on two sides, while the asymmetrical arrangement may be described as "off center." Symmetrical balance tends to be rather formal, with one side the mirror image of the other. Asymmetrical balance comes mostly from the ikebana influence in floral design. It is composed of a comparative equivalent of volume and weight so that placement on one side is equal to placement on the other side of the design, while not being exactly the same.

Rhythm in a design is the appearance of motion, due to the attraction of the eye from one point of interest to another.

Focal point is simply an area in the design where all of the converging stems, colors, and materials create an interest that attracts the eye. It is not a bulls-eye, but a means to bring interaction of all lines together.

You need not be afraid of your materials. Look at the way flowers and plants grow; study their form, textures, and color. Nature is one of our best teachers. Learning to control the material so that it can be expressed in a pleasing, natural way in the design, brings the ultimate success in flower arranging.

Floral designing need not be intimidating. It is: establishing a pattern; studying your materials; putting them together according to a plan. When this is done, a successful design is created.

Ralph Null, AIFD, AAF, PFCI
Professor of Floral Design and Landscape Horticulture
Mississippi State University, Mississippi

Professor Null is a Past President of the American Institute of Floral Design. He holds workshops throughout the United States; he has been a featured guest-speaker in Europe, Africa, Japan, Canada, and Mexico.

Professor Null is currently preparing a full-length book dealing with this subject. We are grateful to him for offering to share some of his expert knowledge with the readers and viewers of the flower shop.

Introduction

The creative urge is one of the strongest that we humans experience. Acting on that urge is rewarding and fulfilling. Have you ever considered the notion that working with flowers and plants is creative, therefore artistic? Any time you develop something, whether it be writing, painting, dancing, or designing, or put something of yourself in a work, you are creating; *you* are the artist.

The goal of *the flower shop* is to help you explore your creativity through floral designing. To help focus your creativity, this volume explains some basics of floral arranging. By going through the stages of our designs, we hope to help the inexperienced flower arranger answer some questions. In fact, the entire television series and this companion book are planned around such questions as: "How do I learn to do a floral design?" "Which flowers are best for a lasting arrangement?" "What types of tools should be used for floral designing?" Each chapter focuses on a different theme and addresses some of these queries.

The floral designs seen on *the flower shop* are illustrated in this book. A pictorial guide and corresponding step-by-step instructions will enable you to produce all 26 arrangements seen on the show.

So, read on, and learn to express yourself by working with this particular medium. We encourage you to take the ideas and information from this book and begin experimenting on your own. Floral designing can be a pleasant, creative experience and a satisfying pastime.

Welcome to...*the flower shop*.

1

Be an Artist

Throughout this book, we will encourage you to consider yourself an artist, and explore creative horizons. In order to do that, you will no doubt do as the artist does: inquire, seek, learn. Let us help you begin....

One of the most common questions asked by people new to floral designing is which flowers to choose. The answer, of course, largely depends on the occasion and the intended use. There are some flowers, however, that can always be counted on—what the floral industry calls "standbys." Standbys or "dependables" are called that because they have such a long vase life when properly treated and placed in an arrangement. (See details relating to care and handling of fresh materials in Chapter 2.)

There are several types of readily available standbys. The first type is a member of a very large family, the chrysanthemums. Some species of the crysanthemum family, such as snow crystals, are referred to as "pompons" because they have multiple branches with flowers on a stem. This is also called a *spray flower*. Another extremely long-lasting flower, which can be used as an accent in design, is statice. The statice actually dries in place, enabling you to use it in two or three arrangements or to pull it out and use it in a silk or dried arrangement.

Statice can also be used to add bits of color to your potpourri of dried petals.

Carnations are another type of standby. The carnation is America's most widely used flower, despite the fact that the rose is now honored as our national flower. Carnations are popular because they are readily available and dependable. The most familiar carnations are the full-size standards. There are also miniature, or pixie, carnations. These also come as a spray of flowers as previously described. Another type of carnation that is gaining popularity is the Chinese miniature. Chinese miniatures are smaller than the pixies and their color combinations and serrated edges offer a little more complex pattern. These popular standbys, carnations, are the focus of the following two basic arrangements.

RESOURCE DESIGNERS

Mr. Phil Easter, AIFD, AAF, PFCI
Montgomery, AL

Ms. Peggy Horne
Winter Springs, FL

Pink Triangle Arrangement

Multi-purpose Conical Design

Pink Triangle
Arrangement

Prepare the foam and container as directed on page viii. Visualize the most outward limits of the planned arrangement. Establish the boundaries of the arrangement by placing the top-most—the highest reaching—flower first. Insert the stem of the first flower vertically into the rear center portion of the foam. Next, place the two lowest flowers one on each side of the triangle; insert the stems at a slight angle into the foam just above the lip of the container so that the flower heads hang out below the lip (**Figure 1**).

Figure 1

To determine the front to back depth of the arrangement, place a flower at the front center of the foam just above the lip of the container with the bloom positioned below the container lip. To complete the triangular outline, place additional flowers in line with the first boundary flowers.

Figure 2

Use all of the additional flowers to fill in the three-dimensional triangular shape of the arrangement. In order to fill out the design and make it more interesting, place flowers at various levels and depths. If a flower is too long or is placed incorrectly, remove the flower from the foam, recut the stem, and place the flower in a different hole in the foam. Do not place another flower in that first hole, or that flower will not live as long as it should. That is because trapped air interferes with the water traveling up the flower stem and causes the bloom to wilt more quickly.

Figure 3

Figure 4

Addition of Foliage

Choose some leather leaf fern to give color contrast and textural variety in filling out your arrangement. Carefully cut the fern to the desired length and insert into the floral foam, beginning at the lip of the container. As with the carnations, place the fern so that it drapes over the edge of the container. This is called breaking the edge of the container. This technique helps to join the flowers, foliage, and container together. Make sure that you do not lose the triangular shape of the arrangement.

Fill in the balance of the arrangement with the foliage, making sure that you conceal the foam and tape. If the arrangement is to be used against a wall, reverse one leaf of fern at the top of the arrangement to give a definite, flat background to the arrangement. This prevents the viewer's "eye" from wandering through the arrangement to the wall. If, however, the arrangement is to be placed in front of a mirror, the rear top piece of fern is placed front surface forward. The gentle curve of the foliage will lead the viewer's "eye" through the arrangement, into the mirror, and back into the room.

Mist the finished arrangement with water. Fill the container with a solution of water and preservative. Slip the arrangement into a decorative container of your choice.

Multi-purpose Conical Arrangement

This arrangement is ideal for a centerpiece. Unlike the triangular arrangement, this design looks complete from any angle.

Prepare the foam and container as directed on page viii.

First, establish the boundaries of your arrangement. Insert the tallest flower at the direct center of the foam. This flower should not exceed 14" in height, as this has been determined to be the "magic height" for avoiding blockage of dinner conversation across the table. If your flower is too tall, remove it, cut the stem, and place it in a different hole in the foam. Establish the baseline of the arrangement by placing five or more flowers around the lip of the container, to form the circular base. Three flowers tend to result in a triangular base and four flowers result in a square base. Place the base flowers at slightly different levels to give more visual interest to the arrangement.

Figure 1

Figure 2

Figure 3

Figure 4

Place the remaining flowers at various levels to define the three-dimensional conical shape of the design. Using leather leaf fern, fill in the spaces between the flowers. Be sure to place enough fern at the base to cover the foam and tape, known as the mechanics of arranging.

Now experiment with your design by using various foliage, baby's breath, or other flowers to fill out your arrangement.

Mist the arrangement with water, add a solution of water and preservative to the container, and place the finished arrangement in a decorative container.

The resourse designers for the carnation arrangements in "Be an Artist" are Mr. Phil Easter, AAF, AIFD, PFCI of Montgomery, Alabama and Ms. Peggy Horne of Winter Springs, Florida. In addition to starring on *the flower shop*, Mr. Easter travels extensively in his capacity of Professional Floral Commentator. Ms. Peggy Horne is the Floral Design Coordinator for the television series *the flower shop*, and floral consultant to major hotels in Central Florida.

GLOSSARY

Floral adhesive tape: This tape is strongly adhesive and is used primarily to anchor floral foams, chicken wire, etc. onto containers. This tape is NOT the same as floral tape.

Floral preservatives: Usually is readily available wherever flowers are sold. Many florists include small packets of preservatives with purchase of fresh flowers.

The role of preservative is to extend the vase life of fresh flowers by: (1) providing a source of food, mainly sugar, (2) keeping the water absorbing channels in the flower stem open, so that water can more readily enter the flower head, and (3) reducing bacteria in the solution that can cause clogged stems and unpleasant odors.

Mix with warm water (100-115°) as directed on the preservative package.

Use of commercial perservatives is very strongly recommended. If not available, however, adding a bit of sugar to warm water will provide some food source, while a few drops of laundry bleach will help control bacteria.

Floral tape: A light-weight, slightly adhesive tape used in the assembly of corsages, boutonnieres, and flower stems. It is also used to cover florist wire. Floral tape comes in several colors, the most common being the stem colors light green, dark green, and khaki.

Leather leaf fern: Has fronds that are 8"-16" long. It is a long lasting fern when provided with a constant source of water. Slightly shiny, the fronds are easily cut into smaller sections as needed. Vase life is 7-14 days.

Utility containers: Containers designed to meet a need, to hold flowers. Generally made of nondecorative plaster, metal, glass, or maché, they are usually inexpensive.

2

The Rose:
Our National Flower

In 1986, the rose was named the national flower of the United States. That's especially appropriate, as the rose can be grown in all 50 states and can be found in most gardens. Of course, the most famous rose garden is on the White House grounds, a fitting tribute to our national flower.

Roses can be grown in almost any garden or purchased at a supermarket, flower stand, or from a local florist. But few people understand how to properly care for fresh-cut roses. Properly cared-for roses can last anywhere from 4 to 7 days. Following are some tips for longer vase life for roses as well as other fresh flowers:

1. If your roses come arranged in sponge-like foam or other filler material, add water immediately but slowly to saturate the filler. Then, add water daily to keep as much of the filler under water as possible.

2. If your roses are delivered loose in a box, they have been out of water for a period of 1 to several hours. It is very important that you "condition" these flowers promptly and properly. If this vital task cannot be performed at once, keep the roses in a cool, dark place, but NEVER in a freezer.

3. It is preferable to "condition" roses (and all other flowers) before actually doing an arrangement. First, carefully remove all foliage and thorns that will be under water during the "conditioning" process. Do this with a sharp knife, being careful not to scrape the green bark of the stem. Next, remove the lower 2" of stem with a sharp knife or shears, ideally with the stem underwater in a solution of floral preservative and warm water (100-115°). This eliminates a rush of air into the stem, which could form a blockage, thus reducing and slowing the uptake of water into the stem. Roses that receive sufficient water have strong stems and are turgid. Next, place the roses, in the preservative solution, in a cool, dark place for an hour or more, but never at sub-freezing temperature.

Floral preservatives are available at your retail florists. Mix with warm water, as directed.

(Continues on page 16.)

RESOURCE INFORMATION

ROSES, INC.
Haslett, MI

Traditional Rose Arrangement

Five Elegant Roses

Traditional Rose Arrangement

This traditional arrangement of a dozen roses is appropriate for most occasions and is always well-received. This design is not difficult, but proper preparation is necessary to ensure an attractive and long-lasting arrangement.

Remove excess foliage from the bottom ¾ of the stems of all roses. Cut the bottom of the stems diagonally. Make the cuts under running water or in a pan filled with water that has been treated with preservative. Refer back to the beginning of this chapter for more complete information on care and conditioning of roses.

Fill the vase with a solution of floral preservative and water. The preservative can be purchased at any craft store or florist.

Partially fill the vase with leather leaf fern in a collar effect, as shown in **Figure 1**.

Figure 1

Figure 2

Figure 3

Now place the roses in the vase, placing the tallest rose at the center and shortening the roses by ½"-1" gradations as you make placements toward the outer perimeter of the vase (**Figure 2**). This will allow the arrangement to be viewed from any side.

The rose placement is now complete (**Figure 3**). Add pink wax flowers, heather, or baby's breath to fill in and add interest to the arrangement (**Figure 4**).

Figure 4

Five Elegant Roses

Begin with a rectangular container that is approximately 8" x 4" wide and 2" deep. We chose a black container, but another color of your choosing can be substituted.

Place a prong into the left rear corner of the container. Secure the prong with floral adhesive. Add a small piece of foam that has been soaked in preservative-treated water to the prong. Make sure the foam is well-saturated. Place two pieces of curly willow to the left and right of the foam, as shown in **Figure 1**. Next add huckleberry and ivy to the design in a placement like that of **Figure 2**. Insert a piece of Boston fern into the front right portion of the foam. The fern should extend on a diagonal to the right, coming over the lip of the container (**Figure 3**).

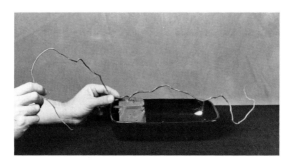

Figure 1

Figure 2

Place the first rose, which should be cut approximately 12" long, in the left, rear corner of the foam. Cut the second rose about 3" shorter than the first, and place it in front of the first rose. Work forward, placing your roses from the back to the front of the foam. **Figure 4** shows the correct placement of the remaining roses.

Insert sprengeri fern, if needed, to fill in large spaces. Use mosses to cover the foam. To complete the arrangement, add a votive candle to the front right section of the container. This adds interest, movement, and light to the arrangement.

Figure 3

Figure 4

(Continued from page 9.)

4. If a rose appears to be wilting upon receipt (or after having been in an arrangement for a day or so), you can revive it by recutting the stem, again underwater (see number 3 above).

Should the flower be severely wilted, re-cut as described above, then lay the entire flower under water in a sink or tub. If the stem is bent, gently straighten it before submerging the flower. When the rose revives, after an hour or two, it can then be arranged or returned to the design from which it was taken.

Should the rose stem be too far deteriorated for revival, cut the flower head from the stem and float it in a shallow bowl of warm water and preservative. It can still be enjoyed in this manner.

5. Keep roses away from direct sun and drafts and put them in a cool, dark place at night (remember, never freeze). Do not place an arrangement of roses (or any other flowers) on the TV, radiator, or any other heat source.

Few things in life express your thoughtfulness and generosity so beautifully and so simply as roses. By following these few simple tips, your roses will be a lasting token of affection for any occasion.

GLOSSARY

Baby's breath (Gypsophila): A popular and readily available fresh or filler flower. Normally found in white, it is also grown in pink. As a dried material, it acts as a long-lasting filler in either fresh or dried arrangements. Vase life 5-7 days fresh, 1 year dried.

Boston fern: A popular house plant for generations. Along with a shorter relative, sword fern, is increasingly popular as foliages for fresh arrangement.

Curly willow: see page 40.

Heather: Pinkish-purple flower cluster from a low-growing shrub. Used in fresh and dried arrangements as fillers.

Huckleberry: A glossy-leaved, branching foliage with woody stem often used in fresh arrangements. Red huckleberry, with smaller reddish leaves of the same shape, but much more vertical and less branching, is used as a "line" material.

Mosses: see page 40.

Prong: see page 40.

Sprengeri fern: A feathery, trailing fern often used in fresh floral designs. Ideal for adding length to arrangements, it is sometimes 30" or longer.

Wax flower: A filler flower with small stiff wax-like flowers on somewhat woody stems. Long-lasting in fresh arrangements. Usually found in a soft lavender color.

3

Impromptu Entertaining

Gatherings that are put together at the drop of a hat are often frustrating due to time constraints. But they can also be the most fun, and flowers help make even the most hurried of gatherings seem planned. If you think flowers, and combine them with a theme or mood, you can create lasting memories for your family or friends.

Occasions for an impromptu celebration may vary, but whether it is a bon voyage party or a celebration of spring, flowers add a special touch. We have some general suggestions that might trigger your own ideas.

For an elegant design, use individual pin holders to exhibit candles and fresh flowers. Using candles and flowers together in the same container rather than side by side is an exciting combination. The flowers and candles can be placed in one main focal piece design, or in individual miniature arrangements. Allow this "group of designs" to cover the entire length of the buffet or dining table.

Match your table coverings to the theme of the holders and flowers. Are you using glass, silver, and elegant flowers? Picture lovely roses or mini-carnations in this setting, placing them on a long glass mirror or linen runner.

Are you using paper plates and cups? Try wild flowers in rattan and placed on a burlap or cotton runner. How about an inside picnic? Recreate a rustic mood using stoneware or earthen materials and heavier colored candles. Place them on textured "earth tone" fabrics. Runners, by the way, are easy to make at the last minute. The right kind of fabric can simply be cut and fringed to create the desired look. Avoid delicate flowers in such designs, seeking instead to include flowers suitable to your natural or rustic theme. Depending on the time of year, you might use Gerbera daisies, in orange, for example.

How about using silk and dried flowers in textured holders, resting on a tweed runner? Also, shawls or large scarves can be brought out of retirement from the cedar chest and pressed into immediate service as an accent covering for a table.

(Continues on page 24.)

RESOURCE DESIGNER
Mr. Tom Powell, AAF, AIFD
Washington, D. C.

Multiple Candle Arrangement

Indoor Succulent Garden

Multiple Candle Arrangement

Place five 15"-18" taper candles in the refrigerator overnight. This will extend their usefulness by enabling them to burn more slowly. After removing the candles from the refrigerator, put the bottom 1" of the candle into warm water to soften slightly. This will prevent the candle from splitting when pressed into the pinholder.

Obtain several 2"-4" pin-holder cups. We chose five cups for this arrangement, but you may use more or less depending on the amount of space you have available. If pin-holder cups are unavailable, another small container may be substituted. In this case, secure a plastic prong in each container with floral adhesive. Place a small block of foam on the prong in each holder.

Place each candle into the center of the pinholder, or foam, as the case may be. Push lightly to secure candle.

Now cover the foam or pin-holder with moss (**Figure 1**). Add a single galax leaf to the front right corner, as shown in **Figure 2**.

Figure 1

Figure 2

Figure 3

To the middle of the left side add two to three stems of cut nerine lilies, as shown in **Figure 2**. Place the base of the stems close to the candle, but allow the flower tips to reach over the edge of the container (**Figure 3**). Add a stem of statice that is a few inches shorter than the candle to the rear of the nerine lilies and the left of the candle (**Figure 3**).

To complete the design, add two or three roses to the design. The tallest flower should be slightly shorter than the candle. An additional flower should be placed at the bottom of the arrangement, so it appears to rest on the galax leaf (**Figure 4**). Other flowers, such as geranium buds, can be substituted for the roses. If you are using longer stemmed flowers, remember to angle the stem outward, away from the candle to avoid burning the flower.

Group the individual arrangements as is appropriate for your setting. This design can be displayed on a tablecloth or runner, or on an oblong bevelled mirror for an extra special occasion.

Figure 4

Indoor Succulent Garden

The container for this arrangement is a clay cactus pan that is approximately 18" in diameter and 4"-5" in depth.

Place a piece of dry floral foam lengthwise into the back of the shallow container. Secure the foam with hot glue or floral adhesive.

Insert a piece of driftwood, which is at least four times the height of the container, vertically in the foam, as seen in **Figure 1**. Secure the driftwood in place with wire or hot glue.

Place charcoal chips into the bottom of the container to keep the sand or soil sweet. Add sand or soil to within 1"-2" of the top of the container. Fill the rest of the container with colored cork in a color that will complement your decor. We chose gray cork.

Insert cacti or succulents according to personal preference randomly in the container (see **Figure 1**). Sparingly distribute charcoal in a design that is appealing to you.

Now attach echeveria and string of pearls succulent to the top of the driftwood, allowing it to cascade from the top. Use a hot glue gun or other appropriate craft glue to make sure it is securely attached. Add deer moss or lichen for interest, as shown in **Figure 2**.

Figure 1

Figure 2

Figure 3

Figure 4

Next wedge a votive candle that is in a glass votive cup in among the sedums (**Figure 3**).

Place a piece of curly willow that is about twice the height of the driftwood in the back of the foam, to the left of the driftwood. The curly willow should lean to the left to balance the arrangement. Glue a piece of Spanish moss to the end of the curly willow (**Figure 4**).

To extend the design, place votive candles in smaller clay pots. You can also place individual sedums in small clay pots. Group these in small clusters, mixing candles and sedums.

The resource designer for "Impromptu Entertaining" is international designer Mr. Tom Powell, AAF, AIFD. He is the owner of Flower Gallery, Washington, D.C. Mr. Powell was the Chairman Floral Decorations for Inaugural Balls and two galas for President Reagan's 1984 Inauguration. He was also the Floral Design Coordinator for the rededication of the Statue of Liberty. He is Past President of AIFD.

(Continued from page 17.)

Clay pots, filled with foliages and grouped on the dining table, end tables, or stair case make a dramatic room. Tie braided autumn-colored ribbons around the pots, and place a single fresh flower in only one or two pots in each group.

Some daring hosts and hostesses have used costume jewelry as accents to their designs. Such pieces make designs unique, and if eclectic is your piece of cake, go to it! Try to find a common theme to tie your arrangements and your party together. Speaking of ties: long ribbons or cords, chosen to compliment the color scheme and theme of the party, can be attached to items throughout your party area or dining area. When the cord is tied, add a lovely fresh flower. Place the flower in an aquapic or tape a bit of wet cotton to the the end of the stem and cover with a piece of foliage so that the flower will be beautiful all evening.

So enjoy! and make your own rules. Keep in mind the brief preliminary care you've learned to give to the fresh flowers you are using. Sad looking flowers will quickly "wilt" a party. Beautiful fresh flowers will add welcome zest and be an unspoken compliment to your guests and a final touch to your impromptu entertaining.

GLOSSARY

Aquapic: Normally a clear, green plastic, a pic has a rubber cap with small hole. Will accommodate flower stems of various sizes. The opposite end of pic is pointed and barbed to penetrate soil, foams, etc. If pic is not available, small glass vials with caps will serve.

Cacti: Any of a large group of plants of the family Cactaceae. Having thick, fleshy, often prickly stems that function as leaves. Some species have showy flowers.

Deer moss: Also called Reindeer moss. So named because in the far north, reindeer feed on it. Low, mounding moss of soft grey color. Native to wide geographic area. In nature, very soft. Soften dried moss by submerging briefly in warm water.

Echeveria: Tropical American plant, bearing thick succlent leaves often clustered in a rosette. Commonly called "hen and chicks."

Galax leaves: This long lasting foliage has rounded leaves with slightly serrated edges, in green or reddish colors. In between arrangements, store in a plastic bag in the refrigerator after misting slightly. Ivy or geranium leaves can be substituted.

Hot glue gun: see page 80.

Lichen: see page 80.

Nerine lilies: see page 80.

Pin holder cups: see page 80.

Sedums: see page 80.

Spanish moss: see page 80.

Succulents: see page 80.

Wire: see page 80.

4

The Oriental Influence

The influence of the Orient can be seen in many areas of Western society. Consider the current popularity of Oriental cooking, grasscloth wallpaper, and laquer furniture. All of these things reflect the elegant simplicity of the Far East.

According to Oriental philosophy, man is not dominant in nature, but rather is an integral part of nature, responding to and in harmony with its rhythm. For these people, to be happy is to be in harmony with nature.

This philosophy has affected all forms of Oriental art. To be a painter, sculptor, carpenter, or floral designer is to be the instrument through which nature reveals itself. Whether changing wood into a beautiful piece of furniture or practicing the art of bonsai, the artist's work fosters a greater understanding of nature.

For centuries the Japanese have valued the art of flower arranging. In the 16th century, a Japanese host would often entertain guests in a room where a stylized floral arrangement was the room's focal point. Ikebana, which means flower arranging in Japanese, is an ancient art that is currently practiced by a large proportion of the Japanese population. As with most other Japanese art forms, ikebana emphasizes simplicity and harmony with nature. This method of flower arranging stresses the concept of asymmetrical balance, where each side of the arrangement has an equal amount of volume without being a mirror image. Their sparce use of materials is also symbolic in origin, representing one's understanding of natural balance and order.

Although older than recorded history, the ikebana method of floral arranging, as well as other Oriental art forms involving nature (such as bonsai), can add beauty to any modern or traditional setting.

In our contemporary Western world as in ancient Japan, flowers may reveal much that we can learn if we are to become attuned to nature and enjoy its exquisite gifts.

RESOURCE DESIGNER

Ms. Kiko Zimmerman
Park Ridge, IL

RESOURCE INFORMATION

Ms. Jane Markuson
Orlando, FL

Basic "Seika" Style Design

Rikka (Classic Ikenobo School)

Basic "Seika" Style Design

Place a spiked kenzan (pin holder) in the center of a shallow container (**Figure 1**). We've chosen black; substitute another color if it is more appropriate to your color scheme.

Place one Dutch iris, approximately 18" in height, in the rear center of the kenzan (**Figure 1**). Press firmly to secure the iris in place. Next, place an iris that is 14"-15" tall to the left of the first iris. Finally, place a third iris that is 6"-8" in height in front of the second iris (**Figure 1**).

Place clear marbles in the bottom of the container. It is not necessary to fill the base (**Figure 2**).

Figure 1

Figure 2

Figure 3

Completely cover the kenzan and any open areas of the container with galax leaves or large ivy or geranium leaves (**Figures 3** and **4**). Add water to the container. For a lasting arrangement, this design also can be easily prepared with silk flowers.

Figure 4

Begin with a usubata container, which is an Oriental vase like that shown in these illustrations (**Figures 1-4**). If you cannot obtain a container like this, use something of a similar shape.

Place well-soaked floral foam in the top portion of the container. A kenzan can be substituted for the foam.

Place a lily, which has been stripped of its foliage, to the left rear of the foam or kenzan. The lily should be 2½ times the height of the usubata (or the container you have chosen). The lily should face upward to the left (**Figure 1**).

Figure 1

To the right of the first lily, place another lily. This lily should be 3"-4" shorter than the first lily, and should face away from the arrangement.

Insert a small curved piece of curly willow on the right side of the kenzan or foam. The willow will reach up and extend out over the rim of the container (**Figure 2**). Now select a long dramatic piece of curly willow that is 4 to 5 times the height of the usubata. This piece should be at least twice as large as the first piece of curly willow that you placed. Place the tall piece of curly willow in front of the tall left lily. This willow will also extend beyond the rim of the container, as seen in **Figure 3**.

Figure 2

Figure 3

Add a stem of pompons in front of the shorter lily. Place other pompons closer to the base, as shown in **Figure 3**.

Place two dieffenbachia leaves at the bottom of the arrangement, one pointing to each side (**Figure 4**). Fill the rest of the arrangement with galax leaves or large ivy or geranium leaves to cover the foam or kenzan. The arrangement is now complete.

Figure 4

The resource designer for "The Oriental Influence" is Ms. Kiko Zimmerman, owner of Kiko's Flowers, Park Ridge, Illinois. Ms. Zimmerman was the Head Designer of the FTD Design Team for their 1984 and 1988 Selection Guides. She was also a member of the Japanese team in the 1985 World Cup Competition. She is the Assistant Chairperson for the 1989 World Cup to be held in Tokyo.

GLOSSARY

Dieffenbachia leaves: These leaves are from one of several varieties of Dieffenbachia, commonly called "Dumb Cane."

Dutch Iris: The petals of this iris are much narrower than those of the bearded Iris commonly found in gardens. However, with proper conditioning, the bearded iris could also be used. Most commonly available in shades of blue or purple, they are also grown in yellow and white. Vase life is 3-7 days.

Kenzan: Literal translation: *ken=sword; zan=mountain.* The Japanese term for a weighted, metal needle-point or pin holder onto which flower stems are pushed to hold them securly in place.

Marbles: Clear or colored glass in the traditional round or irregular shapes.

Pompons: Small button-like flowers of some chrysanthemums and dahlias. Depending on variety, pompon vase life is 10-14 days.

Usubata: A classical Japanese floral container. The one shown is actually in two sections. The top section is the water reservoir.

5

Containers as an Art Form

Unique containers and special collectibles can turn the most basic arrangements into successful floral designs. Containers that enhance your environment and suit your personality express your individuality, even when you reproduce the floral arrangements of other designers.

Interesting containers such as pitchers, bottles, and soup tureens can be found in every home. Walk around your home and look for various types of containers. Don't rule out a favorite antique or basket just because it cannot currently hold water. Most containers can be adapted for practical, enjoyable use by adding a water-holding liner. These liners can be styrofoam cups, jar or can lids, plastic bowls or glasses, or even just florist's foil. Liners protect containers from water and chemical damage and hold water in containers that would otherwise be unsuitable for flower arranging.

Baskets are especially appropriate for casual areas. When working with baskets or other coarse woven materials, styles of arrangements should be informal and loose. Basket arrangements make lovely gifts that are not cost-prohibitive.

If you have a variety of bottles and vases with narrow necks, group the bottles together but mix the flowers in each container. Or, for a different look, you can place a single flower in each container.

Use the lids from spray paint cans or mayonnaise jars to make mini-arrangements. These can function as "place vases" to hold place cards at dinner parties.

When you've exhausted the supply of special containers in your home, visit garage sales or flea markets to find an unlimited variety of unique containers. Many times you will find florists have a good selection of containers as well as inexpensive liners. Using interesting baskets and containers will make your designs fun and they will become artistic endeavors. Your choice should only be limited by an inability to fit a liner into a nonvase container.

Selecting an unusual container is the first step toward your artistic creation. So gather all of your favorite pieces from closets or attics and add your mark of individuality to this art form.

RESOURCE DESIGNER

Mr. Wilton Hardy, AIFD, AAF, PFCI
West Palm Beach, FL

Horizontal Design in Antique Box

Country Garden Arrangement

Horizontal Design
in Antique Box

Noncenterpiece arrangements can be placed on coffee tables, end tables, mantles, or against walls. This design is a horizontal arrangement using a decorative metal box from England as the container.

This arrangement is primarily one-sided due to the lid on the box. The lid also places some limitations on the height of the finished arrangement.

Choose an assortment of colored, garden-type flowers. Use at least five different colors and add white as a unifier. For this arrangement, we suggest red miniature carnations, half open pink miniature roses, purple statice, yellow jack straw pompons, blue corn flowers or short delphinium, a touch of orange dried material, and baby's breath. To achieve a soft, airy look add sprengeri or plumosus and leather leaf fern as foliage.

A water-holding liner must be inserted into the metal box because the box is not water tight. The liner is also needed to prevent the chemicals in the preservative and foam from damaging the interior of the metal container. The liner must be elevated using a piece of styrofoam or lumber because the box is several inches too deep.

Place the pre-soaked water-holding foam into the liner with the foam extending 1" or 2" above the lip of the box. Use a short stick or a

Figure 1

Figure 2

Figure 3

Figure 4

6" long wooden pick to hold the box lid in the desired open position. Keep in mind that the interior side of the lid is not decorative and must therefore be hidden with flowers and foliages.

Establish the horizontal boundaries of the arrangement by placing pieces of plumosa that extend out the sides of the box and down to the table top (**Figure 2**). The overall width of the arrangement should be twice the width of the container. Next, establish the vertical boundaries by using foliages or flowers. Now place a red carnation to determine the front boundary of the arrangement (**Figure 3**).

Continue to place flowers to fill in the arrangement, using various stem lengths to achieve interesting shadows and angles. Place one type of flower at a time to achieve an even, well-balanced placement of colors. Add the baby's breath last, using it as a unifying accent throughout the arrangement. Use some of the baby's breath around the outer limits of the arrangement, so that some of the flowers are seen through the baby's breath. Add foliage as needed.

Fill the liner with water. Do not mist because the water might damage the metal container.

Country Garden Arrangement

Into a crock or similar container place pre-soaked floral foam, making sure that it reaches to the bottom of the container. (If the container is not sealed, insert a liner in the opening of the container.) Allow 1"-1½" of the foam to extend above lip of container.

Establish the height of the arrangement by placing a stem of yellow pompons to the center and rear of the foam. The length of the stem should be 1½ times the height of the container. To determine the width of the arrangement, place a stem of miniature carnations toward the rear of the foam on the left side, so that the flower heads hang below the lip of the container. On the right side, use a stem of yellow pompons. To be in proportion to the container, the overall width should be approximately three times the width of the container.

Complete the basic triangular shape by placing additional yellow pompons on each side of the vertical. Insert clusters of bear grass on either side of the vertical pompon (**Figure 1**).

Begin adding statice, and distribute throughout the frame of the arrangement (**Figure 2**).

Figure 1

Figure 2

Figure 3

Add Queen Anne's Lace and delphinium throughout the arrangement (**Figure 3**).

Add sword fern, galax leaves, and additional bear grass. This arrangement will be casual and free-form (**Figure 4**).

The resource designer for "Containers as an Art Form" is Mr. Wilton Hardy, AAF, AIFD, PFCI. He is the owner of Nowlin Flower Shop in West Palm Beach, Florida. Mr. Hardy is the recipient of a national award in design competition, and his design work has been published in national trade publications and selection guides. He has appeared as designer and commentator on numerous panels across the United States.

Figure 4

Curly willow: Sometimes called cork screw willow. A variety of Willow tree with twisting, curving branches. Used fresh or as a dried material, curly willow provides a dramatic, sensual "line" when featured in floral designs.

Liners: Any container that can be used inside another container to hold a floral arrangement. Liners may be a plastic, glass, mache, or other nonporous material, and are usually inexpensive and utilitarian. If commercially made containers are not available in the necessary size, tin cans, jar lids, spray-painted can lids, even heavy-duty aluminum foil may be used.

In the case of fresh flower arrangements, the liner provides a water-tight holder for water and/or wet floral foam and protects containers from possible chemical reactions to the floral foam or floral preservative. With nonperishable arrangements, the use of liners allows us to easily change arrangements in keep-safe containers.

Mosses: Low growing plants found on rocks, trees, moist ground, etc. Varieties differ with geographical area. These tiny plants have very thin leaves with no veins. This means there is no system for transporting moisture and nutrients from soil, etc. into the plant. The mosses actually manufacture their own food internally.

Orange dried material: In this arrangement, hill flowers, dyed orange, have been used in clusters throughout the arrangement for color accent. Other small flowers that serve a similar purpose are bunny tails and star flowers.

Plumosa: A variety of finely-textured asparagus fern. Beautiful when fresh, it sheds badly as it begins to dry. Vase life: 7-10 days.

Prong: Here used to describe an inexpensive plastic version of a needlepoint holder, available in florist or craft stores.

Sinuata statice: Paper-textured clusters of small flowers are actually colorful bracts; within them is a tiny, white true flower at the center. Flower clusters are on branched, "winged" stocks. Wings are actually leaves. Available in purple, yellow, white, and rose pink. Long lasting as a fresh material, and when dried can be added to potpourri for color. Vase life: 7-14 days.

6
Dressing with Flowers

The term *body flower* traditionally conjures up familiar images of shoulder, waist, or wrist corsages. These corsages are classic choices for women, and are always appropriate. However, other more unique options are available. With a little imagination, and some help from the versatile flower, innovative floral interpretations can accessorize any outfit.

For simplicity in preparation, use easily obtainable flowers in season. If you would like to have flowers to coordinate with a favorite outfit, substitute fabric flowers for real ones so they will always be available to you.

For a shoulder or neck corsage, the design of the corsage should compliment the style of the outfit. For example, place a narrow line of rose buds or miniature carnations along a jewel neckline. The flowers therefore become an intricate part of the dress.

A wrist corsage can be coiled, serpentine style, around the arm. It is more interesting and less bulky than a traditional wrist corsage. An ankle arrangement can replace the more common wrist corsage for those who want to emphasize a leg or ankle. Flowers can also be attached to the shoe to make a simple or exotic fashion statement.

Flowers can also be added to an evening purse. Depending on the occasion, the choice ranges from a small, tailored adornment to a more dramatic creation.

A single flower in the hair is always acceptable, and can either enhance a simple hairstyle or add the finishing touch to a dramatic coiffure. For a very formal occasion, a circlet or headband of delicate flowers would be appropriate.

Body flowers should be incorporated into your personal wardrobe for no other reason than it pleases you to wear them. Whether it is a simple, dried lapel flower attached to a business suit or a romantic floral accent calling attention to a trim ankle, body flowers will add a new flare to your wardrobe.

RESOURCE DESIGNER

Mr. Ed Payne, AIFD
Tampa, FL

RESOURCE INFORMATION

FLORIST Magazine
Southfield, MI
THE JOHN HENRY CO.,
Lansing, MI

Alstroemeria   **Cymbidium**

Orchid Corsages

Sweetheart Rose Corsage   **Floribunda Rose Corsage**

Single Orchid Corsage

Cut the stem of an orchid at an angle, leaving approximately 1½"-2", as shown in **Figure 1**.

Pierce the stem directly below the bottom of the flower with 22-gauge wire. Bend the wire to give a hairpin effect (**Figure 2**). Now repeat this procedure with a second wire, piercing the stem 90° from the first wire. This will give strength to the stem. Add wet cotton to the base of the stem, as a water source, to prolong freshness.

Figure 1

Figure 2

Figure 3

Figure 4

Wrap the stem and wire with floral tape (see page 48 for instructions) that matches the color of the flower or the stem (**Figure 3**). Cut and wrap the stems of any foliage that you want to add.

If you are using a commercial water stem, the procedure differs a bit. Cut the stem of the orchid, leaving only about ½" below the head of the flower. The cut must be straight across to give a flat surface into which the chenille stem of the water source is inserted. Make sure that the water source is pressed firmly against the stem. Then pierce the orchid stem with a light weight wire (24-26 guage), folding the ends down along the stem of the water source. Tape the stem with floral tape.

Choose a ribbon to match the flower or the apparel you will be wearing with the corsage. Make a decorative bow with the ribbon (see page 96 for instructions). Secure the ribbon with a pipe cleaner, as shown in **Figure 4**.

Tape all of the pieces together. Cut off any unnecessary stem or form the stem into a curve at the bottom of the mini-corsage.

Similar procedures should be followed to create other fresh flower corsages. For proper wiring of a rose corsage, see Chapter 12, page 92.

Figure 1

Alstroemeria Corsage

Wire and wrap several alstroemeria florets together using floral tape that matches the color of the stem or flower (see page 48).

Position a small flower bud in front of a piece of foliage and tape together (**Figure 1**).

Begin adding other florets and additional foliage. Each time you add a group of flowers or materials, attach to previous group with floral tape (**Figures 2** and **3**).

Figure 2

Figure 3

Attach a bow (refer to page 96 for "Making a Bow") to the main corsage stem, below the last cluster of flowers (**Figure 4**). Tape all of the pieces together and cut to the desired length.

The resource designer for "Dressing with Flowers" is Mr. Ed Payne, AIFD. Mr. Payne is of Flowers Cascade, Tampa, Florida. He participated in the preparation of floral designs for the Inauguration of President Reagan. Mr. Payne is Co-chairman, National AIFD Symposium, Orlando, Florida, for July, 1988.

Figure 4

GLOSSARY

Chenille stem (pipe stem): Readily available in most flower and craft shops, chenille stems can be used in place of taped florist wire when tying bows, etc. Because the chenille will absorb and later release moisture, wet chenille stems can be inserted into the base of flower heads to give a temporary source of water.

Commercial water stem: Consist of a section of cotton-like material that can be soaked in water. The fine chenille tip of the stem is inserted into the base of a flower head, holding the pre-soaked material against the flower stem. These stems provide more moisture than do regular chenille stems.

Floral taping: Good floral tape is slightly adhesive. This aids in holding taped stems together during assembly of corsages, bouquets, etc., without actually binding them together with the tape. (See **Floral tape** on page 8 for additional information.)

A goal in taping wire or stem is to use as little tape as necessary. Stretch the tape before beginning to wrap or bind. (The tape will change color when stretched, usually becoming lighter.) Failure to stretch the tape will result in excessively thick and heavy wires.

Practice by using a heavy gauge wire rather than a thin, light-weight wire. If you are right-handed, hold the wire in your left hand, between the tips of your thumb, index, and third fingers. Stretch the floral tape, then press the end of the tape against the end of the wire and begin to turn the wire with your fingers. Turning the wire, slowly pull the wire away from you, keeping the tape very close to the wire. As the wire turns and you pull tape toward you, the tape will spiral down the wire. Each turn of the tape should slightly overlap the previous one so that the wire is completely covered.

To become more skilled at taping, gradually move to lighter weights of wire.

7

Flowers as Ornamental Options

Flowers can enhance any decorative theme and increase your enjoyment of your personal space, be it at home or office. Floral designs can be used in place of or as accessories to furniture. The entire personality of a room can be altered simply by substituting an appropriate floral design or accessory.

In a foyer or entrance hall, an arrangement of silk or dried materials in a freestanding container or on a stand or entry table welcomes visitors and family alike. A perfect first impression and mood is set by the colors, texture, and form of such an arrangement. Bright, bold, contrasting colors speak of drama and excitement. Uncommon textures and shapes in bold contrast add to the dynamic feel. On the other hand, a relaxed, gracefully arranged design incorporating soft pastels sets a light inviting tone and contributes to a gracious effect. Such an arrangement, strategically placed, acts as a pleasant mood lifter.

What mood do you want to convey in your living area? Calm, restful? Do you intend to encourage a mellow congeniality in the room? Choose a design that will incorporate the natural colorations already introduced into the area. For instance, in a rustic family room, how about a gnarled piece of driftwood and other earth tone accents? Such a design could cover a good portion of a wall, replacing a nonfunctional piece of furniture; or bring it out into the room letting a simple table act as a base for the arrangement. If a stimulating environment is your choice, consider the flair of strong primary colors. Intense hues demand attention and create a focal point for lively conversation.

A floral design itself can be the starting point for your decor. Design an arrangement to your liking and then build around it to create a decor with which you are comfortable. Whether the focal point of a room or an addition to an empty corner, flowers can work to enhance any environment.

RESOURCE DESIGNER

Mr. Randy Baehre, AIFD
Lumberton, NC

Oriental Accessory

Black Earthern Jar with Papyrus and Lilies

Oriental Accessory

Choose a vase that is appropriate for an Oriental design. We chose the vase shown in **Figure 1**, but any similarly-shaped vase would be correct for this design.

Wedge presoaked foam into the vase. If foam is securely wedged into the vase then tape is not needed. This elimination of tape will avoid damage to paint on an antique or special container (**Figure 1**). (An option: substitute fabric flowers, in which case use dry floral foam.)

Lay a long piece of curly willow horizontally across the top of the foam. Press into place and anchor securely with a hairpin-type fastener that is made out of floral wire. (For a dry arrangement, fill the groove in the foam with glue in addition to using the hairpin.) This

will hold the curly willow in place (**Figure 2**). The willow extends well beyond the right side of the container.

Figure 1

Figure 2

Add juniper in the horizontal position at the left side of the vase (**Figure 3**). This will help to balance the arrangement.

Place the stem of the first and longest pincushion protea horizontally in the foam above the lip of the container (**Figure 4**). Follow this with the second and third pincushion protea, forming an irregular, horizontal line (see finished arrangement on page 50) at the top of the vase.

Add mosses to make the arrangement more interesting and to cover the floral foam.

A smaller matching piece can be added. Wedge a piece of foam into a coordinated smaller vase. Allow ½" of foam to extend above rim of vase. Place one pincushion protea off center in the vase, but resting on the foam. Cover the foam with galax, ivy, or geranium leaves. Add one piece of juniper, which extends at a downward angle.

Figure 3

Figure 4

Black Earthen Jar with
Papyrus and Lilies

Acquire a large, black earthen jar similar to the one shown here. Of course, any similarly shaped jar in any color can be substituted. Remember, this arrangement is being created to compliment your environment.

Fill the jar with presoaked blocks of foam. If the jar you chose cannot hold water or is too valuable to get wet, fit a small bowl into the opening of the jar. Tape the bowl into place after filling it with the presoaked foam. This will reduce the amount of foam needed.

Insert a long piece of papyrus into the rear center of the foam. To the left of that vertical piece of papyrus, place two additional papyrus that are bent at 45° angles, as shown in **Figure 2**. Bend each of these stems, placing the upper portion of each stem against and at a 90° angle to the first, vertical papyrus stem. Hold the three stems in place with floral wire pierced through the stems. Clip off the excess wire.

Add calla lilies midway between the two horizontal lines of the the papyrus. If the lilies are not long enough to do this, place the lilies more closely toward the stem of the vertical papyrus (**Figure 2**).

Figure 1

Figure 2

The exotic bulbs

Any unusual plant makes a talking point in the patio-garden or home. Or it can be used for an accent position, such as by the side of a wrought iron gate or in a large tub by a pool. The more spectacular bulbs are ideal for such uses. Some are appreciated for their size, others for their rich fragrance, and yet others for their unusual habit.

Not all of the plants described here are in fact bulbous in a strict botanical sense — some have corms, tubers or rhizomes — but they are all alike in having underground storage organs and periods of dormancy. Bulb merchants group such plants collectively under the umbrella title of bulbs, and they generally need much the same treatment.

With the exception of the lilies, none of the following are reliably hardy in cool temperate climates. Some must be wintered away from frost, and it would be advisable to grow certain others all the time under glass. This of course does not apply in warm climates.

Lovely lilies

Lilies are the aristocrats among bulbs, beautiful in flower, good for cutting, sweetly scented and including kinds for sun or shade. They can be grown cool in pots for indoor display, while some kinds can be forced gently (see page 107).

Some lilies are stem-rooters, and produce roots above the bulb as well as below; so these have to be planted deep enough to allow for this growth. Others, like the white madonna lily (*Lilium*

ed leaves and large, white, t
ti t first appear in
ther colo

need very little covering, although others in this section may require deeper planting. Check such points with your supplier before planting. All lilies appreciate leafy, humus-type soil; some will tolerate lime, others hate it.

Hardiest and easiest outdoors are the European sorts like *L. martagon* (with maroon or white blooms), *L. pyrenaicum* (yellow, spotted with black) and *L. monadelphum* (clear yellow with black spots). Among the oriental species is the splendid *L. auratum*, with immense flowers up to a foot across, white, streaked with gold and crimson; *L. henryi*, orange; *L. regale*, richly scented and creamy-white; *L. speciosum*, with white or crimson reflexed flowers; and the fiery-gold *L. tigrinum*, the tiger lily.

Lilium candidum

Hybrid lilies are sold as garden or pot-plants, and are more disease-resistant – especially the Mid-Century group, the de Graaf lilies and the Preston and Bellingham hybrids. The best kinds for forcing are the Mid-Century hybrids, *L. auratum*, *L. speciosum*, and *L. longiflorum* (the Easter lily, with white, heavily fragrant blooms that – in spite of the name – appear in summer).

Long-flowering exotics

Agapanthus are used freely in tropical gardens, but in cooler climates are usually grown in conservatories or in tubs that are stood outside for the summer flowering season. *Agapanthus africanus* (*A. umbellatus*) has strap-like leaves and immense umbels of funnel-shaped, light to deep blue or white flowers on two- to four-foot stems. Very similar and slightly hardier is *A. campanulatus*, whose variety 'Isis' has beautiful lavender-blue flowers.

Light, well drained soil is needed by all *Agapanthus*, with a mulch or feeds in summer and a position in full sun. But withhold water during dormancy. A race known as 'Headbourne Hybrids' is hardier than most and can be grown outdoors in various parts of North America and Europe (including Britain). Keeping the roots protected and dry in winter (with straw and polythene) is the ingredient for success. (See the illustration on page 149.)

Zantedeschia aethiopica (trumpet lily, calla or arum lily) is a long-flowering South African with smooth, arrow-

shaped flowers that in
shaped flowers that in
Other species come in o
example gold in *Z. ell*
yellow in *Z. pentlandii* a
wine-red and almost black
nii. The last is often known a

A form of *Z. aethiopica* ca
borough' is hardy in many
Britain. When in doubt, howev
Zantedeschias in large pots of r
water freely in summer, and
winter temperatures around 10°

Bulbs for pots

Clivia miniata is a favourite c
plant and a robust grower, wit
shaped leaves and huge flower

Freesia hybrids

Figure 3

Figure 4

Add three selloum leaves (or leaves similar in size and texture). Take the stem of the leaf and cut it short to fit closely over the base of the jar. The mid-sized one should have more length and the smallest leaf should be the longest. Place these in the design as shown in **Figure 3**.

Place a conch shell or knot of driftwood at the base of the design. Wrap this natural material with wire and place the wire deep into the foam to anchor the material. To soften the look of the driftwood and make the design more interesting, attach a touch of echeveria to the wood with hot glue (**Figure 4**).

Add moss to the echeveria and cover the foam with similar mosses. This will hide the foam while giving the design a complete look.

The resource designer for "Flowers as Ornamental Options" is Mr. Randy Baehre, AIFD. He is the owner of Lumberton Floral Company, Lumberton, North Carolina. Mr. Baehre is a popular commentator and designer at floral design symposiums. He is *the flower shop's* choice for this subject because of his interest and abilities in the history of floral design as it relates to interior design.

GLOSSARY

Pincushion protea: One of a wide variety of protea, native to Africa and generally found in arid climates. Protea are very long lasting as fresh flowers, and many dry well to provide exotic accents for arrangements of dried materials. Other more readily available flowers suitable for this design are Fuji and standard chrysanthemums. (On our television series, we also made this arrangement with silk water lilies. To recreate, follow directions for the fresh arrangement, only substitute dry floral materials.)

Hairpin fastener: Also referred to as "greenery pins" or "Philly pins," these fasteners may be purchased from floral supply or craft stores. To make your own, bend wire in the shape of a hair pin and snip off excess lengths.

Juniper: A popular landscape evergreen. Because of its linear growth, it is ideal for use in floral design. With a source of water, very long lasting.

Papyrus: An exotic, long-stemmed foliage gaining in popularity. Now becoming more readily available, especially in metropolitan areas.

Selloum leaves: Selloum is one of many varieties of the philadendron family and makes a strong, bold statement when used in floral design. Their leaves are deeply cut or "split" (split leaf Philodendron). The selloums are generally "self heading" or more tree like, as opposed to the vining philodendrons.

8

The Androgynous Flower

A growing awareness of the *individuality* of people has come about in recent years; typical stereotypes are being replaced with a richer, less restrictive view of people.

One result of this developing respect for persons is that flowers are emerging as an appropriate gift for everyone. Afterall—the flower is an androgynous entity; all persons can appreciate and respond to the natural beauty of flowers.

But freedom in gift-giving is just part of the picture. Choosing the flowers appropriate to the particular individual is just as important. Previously, this might have been described as "texture gendering" and we would have considered the masculine and feminine as two extremes. Now, we avoid the inclination to think in terms of masculine or feminine, opting instead to "personality-target." In other words, we look at the individual's personality traits when selecting flowers.

When choosing a floral gift, consider thinking in terms of which colors and textures are suited to the recipient. Color can be a psychological barometer; it creates moods and urges expressions of personality. Advancing or warm colors (i.e., red, yellow, orange) are generally associated with an outgoing person. Receding or cool colors (i.e., green, blue, violet) bespeak a private nature.

Drama and excitement are called into play when warm colors are used. Tranquility and relaxation are induced by the cool neighbors on the color wheel.

In the same way, textures are used to express personality types. In the case of plant or flower materials, coarse or rough petals or foliage are indicative of the bold or assertive nature, formerly assigned to men. On the other hand, smooth, fine flower materials are representative of the quiet, gentle individual, heretofore considered feminine.

Old gender generalities are no longer acceptable. The emphasis is on the individual and his or her persona. So, consider the nature of the person who is receiving your gift, and let your intuition and these simple guides help you as you tailor your floral gift to each individual.

RESOURCE DESIGNER

Ms. Frankie Shelton, AIFD,
AAF, PFCI
Houston, TX

Monochromatic Vertical Design

Trellis Arrangement

Monochromatic Vertical Design

Begin with a 12" or taller cylindrical vase. Place two or more well-soaked pieces of floral foam into the container. Make sure that the foam reaches all the way to the bottom of the container, providing a constant source of water. The foam should also extend upward approximately 1" above the rim of the vase.

Toward the rear center of the container, place two pieces of river cane or papyrus vertically into the foam. The length of the cane or papyrus should be about 2½ times the height of the container (**Figure 1**).

Place galax leaves over the foam at the base of the arrangement.

Insert a vertical piece of huckleberry green behind the river cane or papyrus. Next, insert a group of trimmed bear grass to the left of the cane or papyrus, creating a fan effect (**Figure 2**). Now place some more huckleberry foliage on a strong, horizontal line to the right of the arrangement.

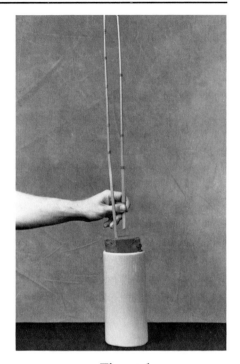

Figure 1

Figure 2

Insert pink nerine lilies to the right of the cane or papyrus, as shown in **Figure 3**. Place pink tulips in a cluster in the right lower segment of the arrangement. Place the last tulip horizontally. Note that tulip stems continue to grow after being cut, so take this into consideration when placing each tulip bloom. To complete the design, add foliage as needed (**Figure 4**).

Figure 3

Figure 4

Trellis Arrangement

Begin with a bamboo basket. Add a plastic liner to the basket since it is not a water-holding container. Fill the liner with well-soaked floral foam, which extends upward approximately ½" above the rim of the liner.

Using raffia, tie together three pieces of pussy willow to form a trellis, as shown in **Figure 1**. Insert the trellis into the middle of the foam.

Next insert one stem of a yellow flowering lily, which has been stripped of foliage, into the center rear of the foam. Place a second stem of lilies to the left of the first one. Now place two more shortened lilies at the front base of the trellis (**Figure 2**).

Figure 1

Figure 2

Figure 3

Add Boston fern behind the right side of the pussy willow trellis. Place plumosa behind the lower lilies and in front of the trellis to fill-in the design.

To complete the arrangement, place a white lotus pod or other decorative pod to the right of the lower lilies. This will add contrast and give a finished look to the design (**Figure 4**).

The resource designer for "The Androgynous Flower" is Ms. Frankie Shelton, AAF, AIFD, PFCI. Ms. Shelton is the Director of the Shelton School of Floral Design in Houston, Texas. She is an international commentator and designer, and received the Distinguished Service Award for the Floral Industry in 1985. Ms. Shelton was a designer for the 1985 Inauguration and Liberty Weekend, 1986.

Figure 4

GLOSSARY

Androgynous: By definition, both male and female in one. In botany, bearing both staminate and pistillate flowers in the same inflorescence or cluster. We have used the term to refer to the suitability and acceptability of flowers for both men and women.

Asiatic Connecticut king lilies: A variety of yellow lilies belonging to type classified as "Asiatic," or hybrid of tiger lilies. Vase life of each open flower is 4-5 days.

Bear grass: Long, thin, gracefully draping foliage. Several pieces of bear grass can be held together by a wired wood pick for ease of use in an arrangement. The base of the leaves should go into the water-holding foam. In dried arrangements, a possible substitute would be isolepsis, although the length of this is only about 24".

Decorative pod: In addition to the popular lotus pod, there is a wide variety of pods that work well in floral designs, such as proteas, pine cones, luffa pods, thistles, etc.

Lotus pod: The dried seed pod of the lotus; because of its distinct shape and texture, very popular as decorative accent in floral arrangements.

Personality-target: (As used here and pertaining to floral design.) Matching floral properties to the individual's traits: i.e., bold, distinctive flowers (antherium or king protea) to the dynamic, sophisticated person; garden flowers or natural floral materials to the nature-loving individual, etc.

Raffia: A natural, string-like material used as ribbon or bows in floral design and craft projects.

Texture-gendering: Assignment or association of textures to particular genders, i.e., rough (burlap) or heavy (leather) textures to men; soft (silk) or frilly (lace) to women.

9

Classical Entertaining

By definition, a classical event refers to one possessed of enduring excellence. By incorporating traditional standards and universally accepted principles of style, a classical dinner party can be planned with minimum effort and maximum impact. The floral arrangements can be as simple as a design centerpiece or an intrinsic part of the overall theme.

Begin with a simple plan. After having accomplished the basics for a dinner party, you can then add to it to your heart's content. Since it is always possible to expand on a theme, the completed design can be as complex as you like. Be aware, however, that if you don't have a total picture in mind, it can grow out of proportion.

A good planner will sketch the table in its final stage. Having orchestrated your plans, perhaps by means of a simple blueprint of sorts, you can then list the items needed to carry out its fulfillment.

Following are some general suggestions for the creation of classical events, in this case dinner parties, incorporating flowers as an integral part of your decorative themes.

Glass, crystal, mirrors, and marble create a mood of elegance, brought into being by the refraction of light and clarity of line. In combination with a single color, this can be breathtaking. For example, choose one pastel color for placemats, napkins, candles, and flowers alike. If a formal look is what you're after, all white is an excellent choice. For a highly dramatic effect, peach would do the trick. Imagine an all white table with the only color being a centerpiece of red roses.

Beautiful old silver or china can set the tone for your dinner decor. Don't be afraid to mix patterns. Many fine restaurants do just that. If the effect satisfies your decorative palate it will please your guests too. To enhance the beautiful possessions, elaborate on the "intricate" feel and allow use of flowers in abundance. The oppulence of the Flemish school, using many flowers and colors at will, would be quite appropriate in this case.

Since flowers are so much a part of entertaining, be sure to take time to properly condition them (see Chapter 2 on care and handling). The table will remain lovely if flowers are prepared carefully ahead of time. It is a tribute to you, the host or hostess, to present your floral offerings in top condition.

(Continues on page 72.)

Arrangement with Color Segmentation

Glass and Mirror Centerpiece Design

Arrangement with Color Segmentation

Begin with a round container that is at least 2" deep and measures at least 10" x 8" in diameter. For a formal tone, a silver vegetable dish or silver tray (with adequate lip) would be appropriate. When using a silver piece, protect it with a liner. Place two blocks of well-soaked floral foam into the bowl. Leave a small amount of room on at least one side so that water can be added later as needed. The edges of the foam can be at lip level or slightly higher; the foam should be slightly higher in the center of the container. Carve edges so foam slopes to edge of dish. If using low tray, tape foam in place. Cover the foam with *wet* moss (**Figure 1**), and tuck moss inside dish edges, so water will not run onto table.

Insert approximately five pussy willows in the rear of the foam, to the right of the center (**Figure 1**).

Place six to eight stems of white freesia in varying heights to the front of the pussy willows. Some stems will move through the grouping of willows, toward the rear of the container (see **Figure 2**).

Add two stems of yellow lilies in a grouping to the left of the pussy willows (**Figure 3**).

Now place two or three blue delphiniums in front of, and shorter than, the lilies. Add about five

Figure 1

Figure 2

Figure 3

Figure 4

stems of geraniums to make a grouping in the front of the arrangement. Allow some of the geraniums to cover the rim of the container (**Figure 3**).

Yellow pompons are now placed between the geraniums and the white freesia at varied heights, and placed deep in the arrangement to give depth to the design. Allow some to extend over the right edge of the container (**Figure 3**).

For final grouping of flowers, add ten stems of purple sinuata statice. Place these at a 45° angle on the left side of the design (**Figure 4**).

Add ivy cascading over the rim to the front of the arrangement. Now fill in open areas with sheet moss or deer moss. Add lichens to achieve the garden effect. The design is now complete.

Note that two versions of this design were presented on the television series. The alternate design, which is also segmented and with stronger parallel lines, may be done with similar placement of flowers.

FURTHER NOTES: Sectioning can be at your discretion: six sections for more complex designs, four sections for ease in preparation. Each section will be an individual "planting" of one kind of flower. Begin with tallest flowers, then next shorter, etc.

(Continues on page 72.)

Glass and Mirror Centerpiece Design

Place six pieces of mirrored glass on a table. The glass should be purchased or cut in three different sizes (see **Figure 1**). It should be ⅛"-¼" thick. The glass should be finished on the edges.

Obtain three different sizes of bud vases. The sizes should be in proportion to the sizes of cut mirror.

The flowers may be of various types, but of one color. We chose white and used longifloram lilies, paper white narcissus, bouvardia, Queen Anne's lace, and white freesia (**Figure 2**).

Cut the flowers in three different heights. The tallest flower should be twice the size of the tallest bud vase. The shortest flowers should extend just above the rim of the smallest bud vase.

Figure 1

Figure 2

Mix the flowers as appropriate to the particular containers. See **Figure 3** as a guide for flower placement. Fill the vases with water.

Now place glass pebbles in various places on the mirror to suggest beads of water. Add votive candles to complete the design (**Figure 4**).

Figure 3

Figure 4

(Continued from page 65.)

A good line to follow regarding classical entertaining is this: fall back on traditional values; valid standards of taste are those that have persevered. If you are uncertain about your choices, simplify the design or plans. Again, remember, it's *your* party. If you feel good about your selection and the ambience you have created your guests will, too.

(Continued from page 69.)

(NOTE: avoid having flowers at eye level. Those flowers above eye level should be light and whispy.)

When finishing design, pin small pieces of reindeer moss over the edge of the container (in two places) so that it hangs down slightly. Open areas can have ivy added, which may slightly "trail" onto the table.

Feel free to substitute flowers and floral materials you deem suitable to your particular arrangement.

10
The New Meaning of Wall Flowers

Flowers are a versatile decorative tool, and floral arrangements should not be limited to table surfaces or vases. Don't be concerned if you've run out of ideas in your home or office, because you can move up in the world—up to the wall.

There are many types of wall flower arrangements. Some of the most interesting, yet practical, arrangements are made with fabric flowers or dried materials.

A natural wreath has both charm and beauty. The condition of a grapevine, for instance, will not deteriorate, so it will retain its natural beauty for extended periods. Add dried flowers, ribbons, or yarns to give the wreath color and individuality. Precut styrofoam wreaths can be completely covered with ornaments such as fabric or dried flowers. Grapevine wreaths make unique, personalized gifts.

Common household items can also be used to create wall arrangements. Fabric containers, such as burlap tote-bags, can be attached to the wall and used to hold dried materials. The spaces of a wine-rack filled with floral materials create an interesting design for all seasons.

Fresh materials can also be used to create exceptional wall designs. Flowers and fruit can be combined in special arrangements. Fruit, combined with flowers, make an interesting wall design. Mount foliage and candles on a cutting board, add fresh lemons...and expect compliments from family and guests alike. Artichokes are also easy to work with and are attractive in floral pieces.

When purchasing materials for "wall flowers," always remember the intended use. Some materials can be used outdoors while others, like hand-wrapped silk flowers, can only be used on indoor arrangements. Planning ahead will also help you to shop for all of the needed materials without purchasing unnecessary items.

The possibilities for decorative wall designs are unlimited. So use your imagination and create your own special wall flower arrangement.

RESOURCE DESIGNER

Mr. Brian Benton
Akron, OH

Grapevine Wreath with Lace

Wreath with Mosses and Driftwood

Grapevine Wreath
with Lace

Begin with a preshaped grapevine wreath in whatever size you wish to use. Wrap #40 lace ribbon (this ribbon is about 2" wide) around the wreath "candycane" style. Allow 2"-3" of wreath to show between each strip of ribbon (**Figure 1**). Do not remove ribbon from the bolt before wrapping; move *entire* bolt around wreath, then cut. Repeat with a thinner ribbon for contrast.

Place a 2½"-3" block of dry floral foam at the 5 o'clock position on the wreath. Carefully wrap 22-gauge wire with floral tape. Wrap taped wire around the foam and wreath to secure the foam. (For added security you may wrap taped wire tightly around a wooden pick; prepare a second taped wire and pick unit; wrap both units around the wreath.) Twist the wire in the back of the wreath to make sure it won't unwrap. To further secure the foam, hot glue between the foam and wreath. For additional stability of the foam, you may also hot glue the wire to the foam and/or wrap an additional taped wire around the foam and wreath.

Place a 10"-12" fabric iris into the foam at the back right corner. Place a second fabric iris, 8"-10" tall, in front of the first iris. Place a third fabric iris, which is used as a focal point, into the center of the foam, allowing it to face forward (**Figure 2**).

Figure 1

Figure 2

Figure 3

Begin placing the remaining flowers, following the crescent of the wreath to the left. Vary the length of stems to give different levels of flowers in the arrangement.

You will also need two decorative birds to complete this design. Place the first bird to the left of the iris, facing upward. Place the second bird above the first (**Figure 3**).

Tie a bow approximately 8"-10" across with the lace ribbon and secure it at the 10 o'clock position on the wreath. Use a streamer of the narrower ribbon, attaching one end in each bird's beak.

Cover all mechanics (wire, tape, etc.) with foliage, moss, or lichens. Your wreath is now ready to be displayed (**Figure 4**).

Figure 4

Wreath with Mosses
and Driftwood

Begin with a straw or prefabricated foam wreath in a size that is appropriate for the intended use. Secure mosses of your choice around the front of the wreath with hairpin wire or hot glue (**Figure 1**). Hot glue a piece of driftwood that is suitable for the size of your wreath into place at the 7 o'clock position (**Figure 1**). Use taped wire if extra support is needed. Another decorative element may be substituted for the driftwood.

Take a dry block of floral foam and insert taped wire as shown in **Figure 2**; that is, use picks as the base for the wire, and then insert the wire through the foam.

Figure 1

Figure 2

Figure 3

Figure 4

Attach the block of foam to the wreath in the 6 o'clock position by wrapping the taped wire around the wreath and mosses (**Figure 3**). If necessary, add hot glue between the foam and the wreath to make sure that it is attached securely.

Begin inserting dried material such as caspia and flax into the foam, as shown in **Figure 3**. Place the tallest piece of foliage in the rear of the foam, allowing it to touch the top of the wreath. Cover the foam with these materials. Place any kind of dried or silk flower at the bottom right of the foam, with its face pointing forward. This should appear as if the flower was resting on the driftwood (**Figure 4**).

Make sure that all mechanics (foam, wreath, wire, etc.) are covered with moss, pods, or other foliage. Place additional materials wherever you choose, to add interest to the design.

You may not be able to exactly duplicate the design shown here. This type of wreath depends entirely on the types of natural material that are available to you.

The resource designer for "The New Meaning of Wall Flowers" is Mr. Brian Benton. He is the owner-manager of Flowers By Dick & Son, Inc., Akron, Ohio. Mr. Benton was Ohio State Designer of the Year, 1984, and FTD Regional Design Winner, 1986. He was also AFS Regional Design Winner, Detroit, 1987.

GLOSSARY

Dried Protea pods: The dried form of a flower, or sometime the foliage, of one of the extensive protea family of plants. Very effective as exotic dried accent in floral designs.

Hot glue gun: Available in craft stores. You may substitute appropriate brush-on or spray adhesives.

Lichen: Any of numerous plants consisting of a fungus, in close combination with certain green or blue-green algae. Found as crust-like, branching growth on rocks or tree trunks. Many lichens dry into attractive decorative materials.

Nerine lilies: A straight-stemmed member of the lily family with a cluster of several flowers radiating around the tip of the stem, which has no foliage. Most common colors are shades of pink. May substitute other lilies.

Pin holder cups: 2" x 2" square containers incorporating a pin holder. Ideal for small floral accents, multiple unit centerpieces, etc. If unavailable, use small saucers, jar lids, etc. filled with pre-soaked water-holding foam.

Sedums: Any of the various plants of the genus Sedum, with thick, fleshy leaves.

Spanish moss: Plant with grey, threadlike stems, drooping in long, matted clusters. An epiphyte, the moss is an air plant taking moisture and nutrients from the air. Grows in trees in southeast U.S. and tropical America. Sometimes referred to as "old man's beard." Most commercially available Spanish moss has been treated to kill insects.

Succulents: A plant having thick, fleshy leaves or stems that conserve moisture.

Wire: Florists wire is available in a variety of gauges. The larger the gauge number, the smaller the wire; from threadlike #32 to sturdy #16 (called "mum" wire as it is strong enough to support a large standard chrysanthemum).

Wreaths: Wreaths for floral designing and crafts are available in craft stores and florist shops. Seen in a variety of types and sizes, from prefabricated and foam wreaths to straw, grapevine, and birch, wreaths are found in all sizes.

11

The Eloquence of Flowers

Since the beginning of recorded history, people have used flowers to speak for them. A gift of flowers can say anything from "I miss you" to "I'm sorry." Like the changeable chameleon, which seems to adapt to the circumstance, flowers take on the meaning of the moment.

Flowers are a reminder of another's emotions. If you receive flowers upon the birth of a child, you know that the giver rejoices with you. When you suffer the loss of a loved one, you understand that a gift of flowers is meant to convey feelings of sympathy. You know that a special arrangement of flowers often means "I love you" or "Congratulations." It is fortunate that nature provides such a variety of visually pleasing flowers and plants to perfectly communicate the heart's unspoken messages.

Flowers are universally accepted as the perfect gift. So why not also give flowers on nontraditional occasions? Don't wait for a birthday or graduation to present a gift of flowers. Express your creativity through floral arranging, and make someone happy at the same time. They can say "Thanks for working late to help me with my report" or "Great going" to a suddenly studious kid.

The two arrangements described in this chapter fall into the above category. One is a gift to say "Thanks for dinner last night," and the other a gift to say "Nice going" or "Congratulations."

It has been remarked that the flower is like life's own cycle: planting, growing, blooming, withering. Perhaps that is why people relate to flowers so intently. Let their simple eloquence speak for you as you touch others with the beautiful message of flowers.

RESOURCE DESIGNER

Mr. Jason McCollum, AIFD, PFCI

Winter Park, FL

Bird of Paradise Arrangement

Orchid Gift Arrangement

Bird of Paradise
Arrangement

Choose a round container that is at least 10" in diameter and 4"-5" in depth. Secure a spiked kenzan, which is also called a frog or needlepoint holder, in the container with adhesive or tape. Presoaked floral foam may be substituted if necessary.

Firmly press the first Bird of Paradise, which should be approximately 24"-30" tall, into the kenzan at the angle shown in **Figure 1**. The flower should be placed at the 2 o'clock position.

Cut the second Bird of Paradise slightly shorter than the first. Place it directly in front of the first flower (**Figure 1**) and press into place.

Figure 1

The third Bird of Paradise, which should be between the first and second flower in height, should be placed at approximately the 10 o'clock position on the kenzan. The flower should be placed at such an angle so the stems form a "V," as shown in **Figure 1**.

Next, wire a fourth Bird of Paradise in place (at the top of flower stems two and three) in the horizontal position, as shown in **Figure 2**. The flower is attached by inserting wire through both of the flowers that form the "V." Trim the excess wire and tie raffia around the joints to secure in place.

Figure 2

Figure 3

Now wedge a small pineapple into the area at the bottom of the "V." This will add interest and depth to the arrangement. This is illustrated in **Figure 3**.

Completely cover the kenzan with galax leaves.

To finish the design, hot glue a small succulent to the outer stem of the horizontal Bird of Paradise. Next drape a wispy piece of Spanish moss or old man's beard over the stem. This will complete the arrangement.

Figure 4

Orchid Gift Arrangement

Obtain a cutting board that is about 2" thick. This board should have a recessed area containing a stainless steel pan (**Figure 1**).

Affix two plastic prongs to the inside of the pan. Attach the prongs by placing floral adhesive or a similar product, which may be purchased at a florist or craft store, on the bottom of the prongs. The prongs should be placed diagonally across from each other, one on the northwest (top, left) corner of the stainless steel pan and the other on the southeast (bottom, right) corner (**Figure 1**).

Press a well-soaked block of foam onto each prong. The rear piece of foam should be slightly larger.

Spread design cork, which can also be purchased at a craft store or florist, in the bottom of the pan. The cork should cover all of the stainless steel.

Place a Cypripedium orchid (Lady Slipper) in the rear left corner of the foam in a vertical position. The orchid should be approximately 18" tall. A second, slightly shorter, orchid is placed under and to the right of the first orchid (**Figure 1**).

Add a piece of curly willow next to the taller orchid, in the left rear. Placement can vary depending on the pieces available to you. Drape a piece of Spanish moss or old man's beard on the curly willow.

In the front piece of foam, place a third orchid, which is shorter than

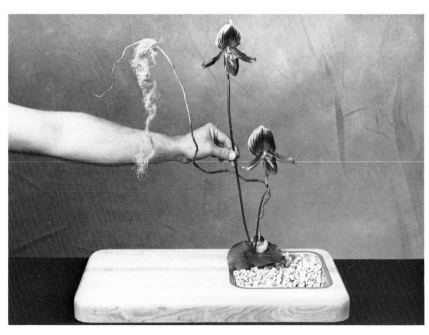

Figure 1

the other two. Place galax leaves at the base of the orchid to cover the foam (**Figure 2**).

Now add two artichokes to the design (**Figure 3**). The stems of the artichokes should be cut very short so that they will rest properly in the pan. The artichokes and pointed lotus pod should be placed as shown in the finished design.

A galax rosette can be made by rolling leaves and attaching them together with floral tape. When the leaves form the desired size rosette, tape the stems together with floral tape. Place the finished rosette in the front left corner of the cutting board. The design is now complete.

Figure 2

Figure 3

GLOSSARY

Cypripedium orchid: Common name, lady slipper orchid. Grown in a variety of colors of green, white, yellow, or shades of brownish red. The pouch, side petals, and top petal are often lined and spotted in a contrasting color. Vase life in corsages or arrangements is 4-5 days if kept cool and misted with water.

12

Flowers are for Everybody

When we think of men wearing flowers we usually think of the common boutonniere attached to a jacket or tuxedo lapel, which are for the most part worn on special occasions, such as weddings and formal functions. Recently men have dared to defy convention and have shed those limitations formerly imposed on them.

We prefer the term *lapel flowers* to boutonniere. The single carnation, the most common type of lapel flower, is still acceptable and pleasant to see, but it is by no means the only acceptable type of lapel flower. To replace the "traditional" lapel flower, here are just a few suggestions for everyday wear:

Three simple stephanotis with ivy
An enchantment lily and lily bud
A mixture of foliages
A spray of fresh or dried heather
A single rose bud on one rose leaf
A mixture of natural materials
  with berries
Silk or dried flowers of any of the
  above

For the more adventuresome, the size of the flower can be increased and various flowers or materials added. As you will see when you begin to experiment, many combinations are possible and moods can be set by the materials chosen.

Along with today's new and attractive menswear, we're also seeing a resurgence in headgear. Men are adding flowers to their hats. A design of natural materials will enhance a simple hat band. The style and size of the floral design should be dictated by the degree of casualness desired. Simple but elegant flowers should be placed on a formal hat, while a casual look could be achieved by a less structured design. Consider using some of the simple lapel flowers, mentioned earlier, as hat flowers.

Men have long been free to wear traditional boutonnieres, but, as you see, their options have expanded greatly and now include a variety of possibilities.

RESOURCE DESIGNERS

Mr. Phil Easter, AIFD, PFCI
Montgomery, AL

Ms. Peggy Horne
Winter Springs, FL

RESOURCE INFORMATION

FLORIST Magazine
Southfield, MI

The JOHN HENRY CO.
Lansing, MI

Rose Lapel Flower　　　Lapel Flower with Dried Materials and Sedum

Lapel Flower of Silk and
Dried Materials

Lapel Flower of Fresh White Lilac

Rose Boutonniere

Begin with a rose in the color of your choice. Cut the stem of the rose at an angle, as shown in **Figure 1**.

Insert a 22-gauge wire that is approximately 4" long through the ovary (**Figure 1**). Bend the wire down on both sides, making a long hairpin effect. Tape the short stem and the wire into place (**Figure 2**), using tape that is as close to the natural color of the stem as possible (see page 48 for taping instructions). Floral tape is available in dark green, light green, and khaki, all of which are generally used for wrapping stems; many other colors are also available.

Figure 1

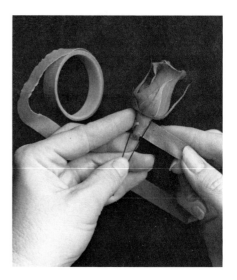

Figure 2

Figure 3

Add foliage as shown in **Figure 3**. If baby's breath or other filler material is desired, add it at this point (**Figure 4**). Tape all foliage to the wrapped wire that is already in place.

Cut off excess wire to complete this boutonniere.

Figure 4

Boutonniere of Silk and Dried Materials

Obtain silk and dried floral materials of your choosing. Here we are working with silk thistles, caspia, and baby's breath.

Cut most of the length of the stems, leaving enough of a stem for you to work with (**Figure 1**).

Using floral tape, tape the wire and stems of the thistles and caspia together (**Figure 2**). The tape should be close in color to the stems.

Figure 1

Figure 2

Figure 3

Add a small amount of baby's breath or other dried material, as shown in **Figure 3**. Tape foliage to previously wrapped stems.

Trim the tape and wire as in **Figure 4**.

The resource designers for "Flowers are for Everybody" are Mr. Phil Easter, Host-Talent for *the flower shop*, and Ms. Peggy Horne, Floral Design Coordinator for *the flower shop*.

Mr. Easter's floral experience, combined with his ability to impart his knowledge to beginning floral devotees, was a major factor in the creation of *the flower shop* series and this book.

Ms. Horne's impressive "back-stage" efforts are visible in our finished programs and book.

Figure 4

Making a Bow:

Select a single-faced or double-faced ribbon: single-faced ribbon has a very definite "front" and "back;" double-faced ribbon is finished on both sides. When using single-faced ribbon, twist the ribbon as the bow is being tied so as to have the front surface always facing outward.

Directions given are for a right-handed person.

1. Begin by pinching the ribbon between the thumb and index finger of your left hand, with 4"-6" of ribbon extending. With your right hand, pull the ribbon away from you, looping back toward your left hand, creating a loop approximately 4" long. Again pinch the ribbon.

2. Pull the ribbon toward you, looping back to the gathering point to create a second loop the same size as the first. Again pinch the ribbon into place. Twist the ribbon back over and around the thumb and pinch, forming a smaller, center loop over the thumb. Repeat to create a second center loop over the thumb.

   Continue to add loops to each side of the bow. Depending upon the effect desired, use three or more loops on each side of the center loops. After the last loop, leave approximatly 6" before cutting the ribbon with sharp scissors.

   Pinch a precut piece of ribbon 14"-18" long, into the back of the bow.

3. To tie off and secure the bow, thread a length of chenille stem inside the center loops but on top of the thumb, then thread the chenille between your fingers. Turn the bow over, cross the ends of the chenille closely against the back of the bow and twist to secure.

   The finished bow has three loops on each side, two center loops to hide the chenille, and four streamers, two longer than the others.

13
Nature in Our Midst

There are two methods or styles that can be used when designing with natural materials. Purist, or naturalistic, designing uses the materials as they are found growing in nature. Leaves are grouped as they would be on a growing plant. Flowers and stems grow upward toward the sun, their leaf surface parallel to the ground to obtain maximum exposure to light; therefore, they are arranged in that manner in purist designing. Other plant materials may be pendulous and cascade or flow from the arrangement. In naturalistic designing, accessory materials would be rocks, moss, twigs, lichens, bark, roots, and driftwood.

Materials that are compatible dictate the design. As an example, in an arrangement made of teredowood (holes are bored by a crustacean) we would also use beechwood, kelp strands, miscellaneous kelp, sand, and succulents.

A purist example would be a bromeliad attached to wood, just as it grows in South America. Another interesting arrangement is a vegetative design with clustering plants and flowers. It should appear as if a specimen was plucked from the edge of the woods in a flowering meadow.

The other style of designing with natural materials is called decorative designing. It allows the use of natural materials that will effectively enhance the floral composition but does not necessarily place them as they are in nature. (If you don't know how something is found in its natural state, then this is the way to go!)

A good example of decorative designing is an arrangement of bare twigs and branches, used with a dozen roses, or a wreath made of vines, mosses, and twigs, with flowers emerging from a central location.

When using the decorative design style, a decorative vase can be used. Beechwood, lichens, and moss, which cover the mechanics and divide groups of flowers, add interest at the base of the arrangement.

When designing with a naturalistic flair, here are some tricks: Clump moss in appropriate places at the base of the design to draw the eye and to cover mechanics. Avoid solid mossing of the container before hand; wait and apply the moss as the final touch.

Polypores (fungi) or small tree conks can be affixed (consider using the hot glue method) to the container or the piece of wood in the arrangement.

(Continues on page 102.)

RESOURCE DESIGNER

Ms. Karen Hobbs Johnson, AIFD
Forks, WA

Forest Garden

Wreath of Mosses and Lichens

Forest Garden

Begin with a large clay saucer similar to that shown here. You may substitute a lighter weight saucer of the same shape.

Pour pieces of colored cork (we are using gray), into the saucer, covering the bottom completely and forming a bed for your arrangement. Now form a design in the saucer by adding black charcoal (**Figure 1**).

Place a piece of driftwood, or similar item, into the rear of the saucer in a horizontal position (**Figure 2**).

Figure 1

Figure 2

Figure 3

Figure 4

Now add sponge lichens, mushrooms taken from logs, or other natural items to the design (**Figures 3** and **4**). These should be affixed with glue. Place these materials in groupings rather than individually. This will make the arrangement seem more natural.

To complete the design, add mosses where appropriate and secure with hot glue.

The materials used for this design, with the exception of the container and cork, will vary depending on your location. Every environment, however, has an abundant supply of natural materials that can be used in an arrangement like this.

The resource designer for "Nature in our Midst" is Ms. Karen Hobbs Johnson, AIFD. Ms. Hobbs is the owner of Hoh Grown, in Forks, WA. She is an expert on the use of natural products in floral design, and is a popular floral commentator and featured designer.

Wreath of Mosses
and Lichens

Begin with prefabricated foam or straw wreath.

Affix mosses or other natural coverings to the wreath with hairpin wire or glue. This procedure is similar to that described on page 78.

Bind a group of scallions with wrapped wire. The wire should be wrapped so it does not cut through the scallions. Attach the scallions to the wreath, at the 12 o'clock position, with wire. Cover the wire with raffia that is tied in the front in a bow. Allow strands of raffia to hang down below the bottom of the wreath.

This design can take advantage of the natural materials available to you in your particular location, or you can seek out specific materials that are reminiscent of geographical areas or seasons you enjoy. (Those we have used are "Hoh Grown" products from Forks, WA, which specializes in natural items from the Pacific Northwest.) For example, a bunch of wild flowers could be easily substituted for the scallions. In autumn, in most parts of the country, groups of colored leaves will add a special touch to your design.

So, let this design inspire your creativity while encouraging you to open your eyes to the natural beauty that surrounds you.

Figure 1

(Continued from page 97.)

Choose materials that look and feel right together. Consider color, shape, texture, proportion, rhythm, motion, etc.

Be aware of the natural items available to you in your area, so you will know what your choices are for your arrangements. When arranging flowers, plants, foliages, fungi, wood, etc., think of groupings rather than of separate, isolated items.

Combine naturalistic principles with decorative design; the outcome is aesthetically pleasing. But remember, in order to create a pleasing design, the material should be organized and suitable for the occasion. You are the artist and creator; if the design pleases you, it is a successful design.

Cover Arrangement

After selecting a large, earthenware or ceramic container, fill it with blocks and partial blocks of pre-soaked water-holding floral foam. The foam should extend 1½"-2" above the top of the container, because floral materials will extend over and slightly down the sides of the container. Secure the foam in place with floral adhesive tape, anchored to the sides of the container.

Choose a piece of curly willow, approximately 2½ times longer than the height of the container. Insert the stem near the rear of the foam to the left of center, extending upward at a 45° angle to the left. To compensate for the left to right diagonal line, insert shorter curly willow into the right side of the foam near the front.

To establish the strong vertical line of the arrangement, select a stem of papyrus at least 2½ times the height of the container. Insert the stem at the center rear of the foam. Place one stem of Amaryllis medcatus in front of the papyrus. Continue the vertical emphasis by placing two tulips in front of the Amaryllis at two different heights, with a tulip on each side of the Amaryllis stem.

To widen the arrangement, on the left side position four to five stems of lilac (with foliage removed) to the left of the Amaryllis. On the right hand side, add a second stem of papyrus and several stems of Boston fern as shown in the finished design.

To emphasize the arrangement's focal area, place a large section of reindeer moss, so that it drapes down over the top of the container on the left side. Moss can be secured with wire formed into hairpins. At the front center of the arrangement place three to four natural or lacquered lotus pods, keeping them in primarily a horizontal profile.

Reinforce the lower, right portion of the diagnoal line of curly willow by adding several pieces of plumosus sprengeri. Use several different lengths to achieve increased visual interest. Finish covering the foam with galax leaves, additional mosses, or other foliages.

Mist the finished arrangement with water and fill the container with a solution of water and floral preservative.

If your container has a lid, it can be placed adjacent to the finished design.

Jason McCollum, AIFD, PFCI, is the designer for the cover arrangment.

Index

Freesia, 21, 68, 70
Fungi, 97. *See also* Natural materials, designs with
Galax leaves, 20, 29, 31, 39, 53, 60
Gender generalities, 57, 89
Geraniums, 68
  leaves of, 29, 31
Gifts with a special message, flowers as, 81-87
Grapevine wreaths, 73, 76-77, 102

Hair, flowers for, 41
Hat band, flowers for, 89
Heather, 13
Horizontal arrangement, 36-37
Huckleberry, 14, 60

Ikebana, 25. *See also* Oriental design
Iris, 28
Ivy, 14, 29, 68

Jewelry as design accent, 22, 24
Juniper, 55

Kenzan, 28-29, 30

Lady slipper, 86
Lapel flowers, 89-95
Leather fern, 5, 7, 12, 36
Length of flowers, boundaries for, 4
Lichens, 22, 69, 101. *See also* Natural materials, designs with
Lilies, 30, 52, 61, 62, 68, 69, 70
Liners for containers, 33, 36, 37
Longiflorum lily, 30
Lotus pod, 63

Marbles, 28
Men, flowers for, 5, 89-95
Messages conveyed with flowers, 81-87
Miniature carnations, 1, 38
  for elegance, 17

Mirror, arrangement to be used in front of, 5
Mirrored glass as part of flower arrangement, 70-71
Mood, flowers to compliment, 17-24, 49, 57
Mosses, 15, 20, 22, 23, 53, 55, 68, 85. *See also* Natural materials, designs with; specific mosses
Mushrooms, 101. *See also* Natural materials, designs with

National flower, rose as, 1, 9
Natural materials, designs with, 97-102. *See also* specific materials

Orchids
  corsage of, 44-45
  gift arrangement with, 86-87
Oriental design, 25-31, 52-53

Papyrus, 54, 60
Personality traits, flowers and, 57
Pincushion protea, 53
Pixie carnations, 1
Place cards, unusual, 33
Plumosus, 36, 37, 63
Polypores, 97. *See also* Natural materials, designs with
Pompons, 1, 31, 38, 69. *See also* Snow crystals
Purist designing, 97-102
Pussy willow, 62, 68

Queen Anne's Lace, 39, 70

Ribbons, 17, 24
River cane, 60
Roses, 1, 36
  in black container, 14-15
  for boutonniere, 89, 92-93
  candles and, 21